AF673742

PASSAGE OF A HEART

POEMS

MICHAEL L. NEWELL

ACKNOWLEDGEMENTS

Many of these poems (sometimes in a different form) have previously appeared in the following periodicals, to whose editors grateful acknowledgement is made: *Bellowing Ark*; *Current*; *The Iconoclast*; *Jerry Jazz Musician*; *Poetry Depth Quarterly*; *Poetry/LA*; *Poppy Road Review*; *Ship of Fools*; *Verse-Virtual.*

I would like to thank the following editors for their many kindnesses over the years: Robert R. Ward; Jerry Austin; Phil Wagner; Jack Hart; Don Wentworth; Firestone Feinberg; Joe Maita; Sandy Benitez.

I would also like to thank the following people for their kindness to my work over the years: Anna and Michael Citrino, David Ellenstein, Robert Fox, Joseph Glaser, Dr. Stellasue Lee, Michael Minassian, Lawrence Noel, Ed Ruzicka, and the indomitable Robert Wexelblatt.

Cover artwork: Michael Citrino
Author Photo: Wendy Keller

ISBN: 978-81-19654-32-1
Tel: +(91) 9415091004 E-mail: info@cyberwit.net

PASSAGE OF A HEART. Copyright 2023 By Michael L. Newell
All rights reserved. No part of this book may be used or reproduced in any manner whatsoever without written permission, except in the case of brief quotations used in critical articles or reviews.

TABLE OF CONTENTS

TABLE OF CONTENTS (PAGE TWO)

TABLE OF CONTENTS (PAGE THREE)

This book is dedicated to the memory of Benjamin Saltman, Don Salper, and Robert Ellenstein, three teachers who had a profound effect on me as a poet, actor, and teacher.

"We make our meek adjustments,
Contented with such random consolations
As the wind deposits
In slithered and too ample pockets."

--"Chaplinesque" by Hart Crane

CONSECRATION

an old couple sat
on battered wooden
porch as a fading

gloomy afternoon
enfolded the pair
while rain strode across

their empty backyard
bestowing blessings
then thrummed upon roof

wild drum sounds unleashed
forgotten rhythms
and boughs rocked and rolled

from windows jazz sang
Ella's voice soothed in
concert with Joe Pass

land trees home music
wind rain wrapped couple
in a state of grace

THE COGNAC OF MEMORY AND IMAGINATION

There is a weariness in things:

> the torn curtain, the frayed trousers,
> the chipped and stained plate, the tattered dress,
> the sagging bookcase, the bent roof fan,
> the three-legged chair, the window
> with a faint crack down its middle;

and there is astonishing life in the stooped couple:

> half blind, partially deaf, they slowly circumnavigate the room, feeling
> memories with their fingers; never the crack, but the child who caused it;
> never the imminent demise, but the living which preceded it; never the rip
> or tear, but the warm flesh in casual contact causing the imperfection;
> all pain eased by the cognac of memory and imagination.

ASHES ON THE WIND

A man stood on Northwest Pacific shoreline,
urn in hands, face to wind,
reluctant to carry out appointed task.

A life contained in vessel filled with ashes,
waiting to be distributed into an uncaring ocean,
seemed insufficient as recognition for 94 years

of being, an existence infused with joy, laughter, great pain,
unanticipated losses, a peripatetic journey with a dearly
loved spouse whose loss leached much of life's meaning.

Now she was ashes in a vase, soon to be tossed onto waves
she had long loved. This was her wish. Nonetheless,
it did not seem enough, this ritual so often performed.

At last the man tossed handfuls into waves, associating each
with a family member. Ashes on the wind
became ashes in the ocean. It seemed inadequate, but necessary.

The wind sang her on her way to whatever future there would be.

AT TWENTY-ONE I CAUGHT THE BLUES

Midnight on flight line,
1966 Oxnard AFB,
I sit in base ops, stare
across darkened runways,
only surly weather officer
as company -- every plane
in its hanger, no one inbound;
half mile away, on freeway, trucks
and occasional car sweep past;

accompanying passages to Ventura
or Los Angeles, lights flicker, lonely
emblems that provide a semblance
of human contact. I lounge in room
large enough to hold thirty people.
Wind sweeps through room. I imagine
Ella and Duke resurrecting Gershwin
just for me; bob my head; shake shoulders;
wind blends with their swinging grace.

I turn from side to side, slow
dance on swivel chair.
I flick on a radio. Wilson Pickett
is singing, "At the Dark End of the Street."
I stop moving. Too lonely.
The room grows chilly. Freeway lights
flicker out, abandon night. Weatherman
leans motionless on counter. When Pickett
finishes, even wind has vanished.

Silence contains voices of family and friends,
many miles away. I am an empty vessel.
Across room weather officer still leans
on counter. He looks at me, shakes head,
disappears into his office. A rat scurries in one door,
out another. I wish phone would ring or someone
walk in. Four more hours until my relief. I can't remember
who I am. Slowly night floats past. Sky turns dark blue.
I hum Nat Adderley's, "Working on a Chain Gang."

When day shift arrives, I greet them with jive.
No one is impressed.

ALL IS ONE, ONE IS ALL

(for Ella Fitzgerald, Nina Simone, and Cleo Laine)

Trumpet and sax sail relaxed
above bobbing heads ensconced
in chairs of velvet comfort,
while bass thrums, and drums
rat-a-tat-tat in this or that rhythm;
the piano knows where the heart
swells and swells before dipping
and diving beneath surging waters
of fellow instruments, and all the audience

in heartfelt agreement lets emotion cascade
into the world, unleashed by musicians
and one singer who opens her heart to bleed
a balm to heal all who play, all who listen,
and to give full expression to a composer's
depth, breadth, sorrow, and hope of future beauty;
a worthwhile concert conjoins all present, stitches
trumpet, sax, bass, drum, piano, audience together;
all made one by a singer through whom life floods;

song has many wings, music fills many hearts;
the only impediments to descant, melody, euphonious joy,
is lack of imagination, arms folded in distrust;
concerts soar when all resound in unfettered unison;
certain women carry all our despair and express it
in unrestrained, full-throated carols of hope wed to pain;
leaving the concert, wind sighs through hair, bones,
and slow moving feet; music's range of beauty requires
attentive silence from all who witnessed its sacred rite.

TALE OF AN UNTAMED TRAVELER

A little gent bopping down a crooked
sidewalk, which turned, turned,
and turned again, ingested snippets

of conversation from passing strangers,
turned their words into imagined dialogues
that he scat sang in rhythm to his

free form jazz steps that enlivened
the passageways he moved along
in a diddley-bop-she-bop slide and glide

that provoked smiles, glares, laughter,
and a hippity-hop bounce from passing
children here and there who created rhymes

in time to the little fellow's strut, sway,
and free form play that so transfixed passersby.
"All movement," thought the little chap,

"is a form of dance, and all dance
is a response to wind, rain, work, play,
grief, exaltation, love, hate, beauty, and hope."

"And all movement and sound provide
the roots of music," he murmured to himself
and whistled an Irish reel, as he clicked his heels.

THIS WAY AND THAT

wind and my hat
in chaotic dance across
city streets
freeform jazz
and I, I swear and bounce
through traffic in clumsy
rollicking pursuit
a drummer who has
lost his sticks

STONED

one two lads and a lass skipped
hopped bounced danced down
a small town street singing a tune
from a generation or more before
they weaved in and out of paths
of their pals singing goodbye Ruby
Tuesday lyrics learned from parents

when they encountered walkers
or bicyclists they parted swerved
and reformed without losing the lyrics
or the rhythms of their ad hoc dance
that made a bright day brighter
I stood and stared as they navigated
the street filled with holiday folk

until they swerved round a curve
out of sight shook my head and set off
for the post office incorporating
an awkward step or two or three
of my own and humming a celebration
of Ruby Tuesday The Stones had done
better than they knew and time flew

LATE IN THE DAY THE MOON AND I

majestic full-blown golden galleon
caught in nearby trees
the two of us alone

in startling moment
a glorious blessing
in fading gloaming

all that is missing
is Miles' horn
in valediction

MOTHER AND CHILD

A woman's fingers explored piano keys,
as though children plowing
through snow drifts in search
of unexpected life;

resulting music liberated birdsong
in trees just beyond her home's windows;
her daughter sat nearby mother's keyboard,
swayed in joyous silence.

Wind rose in accompaniment;
music engulfed the neighborhood.

THE PATH IS SELDOM EASY

No anger, no tears, no recriminations,
deep in sleep, the lass has found peace.
Shadows of trees backlit by a full moon

wash her face as she embraces her pillow.
All strife, those moments when words
are knives, have been blown away

by a midnight breeze, slowly dancing
trees, and the resilience of youth.
The parent slowly sways in concert

with the shadows washing the room,
and prays that tomorrow the teenager's
current peace will carry her joyfully

past the legion of problems that assault
those on the threshold of being adults.
The parent wishes there was a way

to capture in picture or music the silent
harmony the girl unknowingly has found.
How to help her find the way to make

her best moments her path through life?
Leaving the room, the parent recalls
when parental love was so much easier.

THE BLESSING

strolling through the late gloaming
I wander through a small wood
that leads me to a creek where
I discover a young couple leaning
against a large rock their eyes

are upon the stars suddenly a large
moon appears above horizon
I hear the lass say ah Thomas
the moon has blessed your eyes
and turned them golden

their laughter is as rich in sound
as nearby water burbling over stones
and I turn toward home unnoticed
alone yet blessed by being a witness

RIDING THE WIND

a wee lass races downhill
arms flung behind her
hair floating in wild disarray
embraced by the wind
her voice unleashed

full volume into
an indifferent world
her exuberant grin
splits forehead to chin
unaware life waits in ambush

filled with tumbles spills
and bruise upon bruise
for now life means
freedom to dare to spare
no energy nor joy

FREE JAZZ

Wild world of free jazz too often termed autoschediastic,
yet genius of Sun Ra, Ornette Coleman, Mingus, Don Cherry,
mature Coltrane, Cecil Taylor, Pharoah Sanders was both
astonishingly innovative and governed by deep musical insight
and daring of porpoises in uninhibited flight, exploration
rock climbers could appreciate, and spiritual in ways
the most austere monk in a desert cave might recognize.

IN AN EVENING MIST

A raft of ducks, a bundle of bairns, and I
perform an evening dance around a creek,
as Douglas fir trees solo all through
the gloaming in the wind's arms
with a voice like a song softly sung
by Ben Webster's sax. I am wet with joy,
and my companions are free, free, free.

WHO KNEW

The gimp with a corkscrew limp
could no longer dance or move
with grace, speed, or elegance,

but he could blow a horn with chops
that raised young and old to their feet
and spun them like tops, lifted them

into the air with an elevation
that consecrated entire bodies, flesh
freed from shackles, and in his mind

he was still among them, even as he
sat crookedly on a battered chair,
bestowing beauty upon others' flesh

turning a horn into a religious artifact,
his broken body into a conduit for beauty.

SAINT THOMAS AND SONNY ROLLINS

Drummer do your thing, oh yeah, and here comes the man,
Sonny Rollins, hot, wild, with his tune always dancing; lift
your feet, brothers and sisters; feel the imaginative riffs move you
across the world, not floor; this dance covers more ground
than a mere floor tune; its rhythm needs full wild embrace;
that horn leaps up, down, round and round, side to side,
always alive, always finding new things to say; those drums

keep arriving at the right time, in the right ways; wow, what
is that madman seated there doing, so alive, alive-o, and your body
moves, grooves, flies through the air in uninhibited response;
oh, man, shake, rattle, and roll in communion; here comes
The Man back again in full tenor flight; never, never, never,
will you ever find yourself like this without diving into the notes
unleashed by the wild horn driven by the even wilder man;

ah, here comes the piano rippling along over a steady drum
and cymbal beat; the piano reminds us of how mellow things
can be when everything is right with the world, yet still there is that beat
lifting the feet and shoulders; oh my, Mister Rollins is back, and his horn
sings of life, beautiful life, and ends with an emphatic statement of life
everlasting, and its intrinsic worth; when the sound evaporates into silence,
we all are limp as discarded clothing; we slip into chairs, and reflect

on what has transpired over the last seven minutes or so, and smile.

ONE MAN CELEBRATION

A wrinkled face
in a midnight window
ignores all darkened
neighborhood flats,

grins at an owl
flitting past, sings
a children's tune
to rocking chair moon,

imagines his crippled
legs could fly,
and laughs in concert
with spring night wind.

He imagines he lives a joyous
ragged voice blues -- perhaps
true, perhaps not, but wild joy
emanates throughout his room.

CONFESSION

darkness piles round me
foretelling the future coming
steadily closer that will swallow

whatever is left of me as I sit
dreaming of a past never to be

recovered save in corrupted
memory that paints truths
in colors and shapes only

I might consider truth
my mind likely lies as much

as mirrors distort who I am
and have been and night hovers
round all I think and do

A VISION IN THE GLOAMING

a woman caressed
by early moonlight stood
on her balcony

as wind moved clouds
past her lover dimming
and undimming her presence

even in shadows moonlight
lightly stroked her face and hair
and a startled passerby in the woods

blessed her and the oncoming night
who illumined her
all the world felt sacred

and when a light rain swept in
it was holy water

WATER'S MUSIC

Ocean, river, stream, creek,
or falling rain, water always
fills the land with music.

Symphonies, quartets, solos,
classical, jazz, rock and roll,
rhythm and blues, mountain music,

all find inspiration in water's
infinite range of sound, from ripples
to crashing waves, from lapping

at shores, to storm blown currents,
from water roaring through rocks
and boulders, to majestic song

of waterfalls. Music exists wherever
water moves, and attentive listeners
hear its music and its varied beauty,

and musicians open themselves
to all of water's infinite nuances
that let them nourish their creations.

LOOKING BACK

As a high school senior, I loved two things that were
beyond my limited command of language
to adequately share my passions.

The first love was basketball; the second
was classical music, especially Beethoven,
Brahms, and Italian opera.

I would tie my loves together in a wild dance
where I dribbled a basketball all over the family living room
in time to the Eroica Symphony; or I would change

the rhythms with which I dribbled to match them
to a Verdi aria sung by Jussi Bjoerling or Caruso
or Leonard Warren or Renata Tebaldi.

I no longer can control a basketball, doing cuts and spin
moves combined with leaps and sudden changes of direction.
I can no longer sing nor can I make my body part of the music.

I can, though, still hear music in my mind and body when I watch
young athletes create basketball ballets -- some mesh with symphonies,
some jazz, or rock and roll, or blues, but all are alive alive-o,

while deep within there is a movie screen where young men sixty years ago
still pass and cut, fly through the air, create their own visions on faded
black and white canvases, enhanced by distant musical tunes and rhythms.

Walking past an outdoor court, I feel tears forming at the beauty
of young men and women sprinting, leaping, making a basketball
come alive, and want to call a warning that time has them in its grasp.

AS I STAND IN MY DOORWAY

wild wind song
        through cedar and palm
    brings rush of sleet

Beethoven's ghost is loose
        in swelling eventide
    feral music sweeps through the land

I slip inside
        seek a light switch
    I am still in darkness

night swallows us all

WHO AM I TODAY

Sequestered on a bench
beneath pine and palm,
my thoughts are caught
by a breeze and wander
upwards, and I discover
a canopy of blue lit
by brilliant sun rays,
free of clouds and populated

in the distance by kites.
I wonder when it was
I ceased to heed the world
around and above me, glance
down in time to discover
an assembly of ducks
and geese filling a nearby
meadow, joining in

a full-throated cacophony.
Welcome to life, old man,
they seem to say, and I feel
the old desire to wander,
while realizing life is rich
in detail, and exuberance
is everywhere I look.
Hallelujah, I think, hallelujah

for the ducks, geese, egrets,
loons, dogs, squirrels, otters,
and children in ebullient play.
When in the wind, I think,
I should share its freedom
and travel like a congress
of leaves, birds, and porpoises
sailing above the sea.

DUALISM

Wind, rain, sleet endanger me,
as I wander empty streets all through
a small coastal town caught
in a major storm's embrace.

Why am I out here? What leads me
to traverse terrain where weather
could cause me harm, where others
have fled to safety, where most

wild creatures have vanished
into shelter? I lift my face up
into the rain and sleet; I sing old
tunes about facing rain with a strangely

gleeful exuberance, and ignore
occasional passing cars who drench
me as they speed through puddles
that could be small ponds. Why?

Who makes these curious decisions?
Is this truly free will? No idea.
The more I think about this conundrum,
the less I care, and I wander on,

oblivious to surroundings, possible
consequences, or others' opinions.
I spot an otter speeding through
a nearby creek, and I murmur,

"Go brother go, and make this world
a better place." The gloaming
slowly approaches, and the creek's
current sings a joyous welcome.

SECULAR VESPERS

An ancient stepped outside his dwelling
to discover the gloaming was a deep purple,
and a choir of wind was sweeping the landscape.
Ten steps past his door, he stopped, lifted

his face into the wind, and a song formed
within. Geese flocked above, carrying on
a noisy conversation. One last squirrel
disappeared up a tree. The old fellow found

himself smiling uncontrollably, then burst into
celebratory laughter, laughter, and more laughter.
Another elderly chap hobbled past on a cane,
said, "I know exactly what you mean; I love

this time of day; the world is ending and beginning,
all at the same time; lift your arms to the sky."

ALONE

Alone in a room of fifty folk babbling,
rip roaring laughing, punishing one another
with empty caresses, swallowing any available
beverages along with conversations in which
they are blindly immersed, I finally stumble

out a door into windblown, deepening crepuscule
and long for a serenade from Monk, a funky
unpredictable, stumbling, beautiful life-beat
to carry me down the street rediscovering life,

or perhaps find my way through memory's avenues
to a wild, overwhelming dance with Coltrane
at his most chaotic, a roller coaster sonic

exploration of life's dangers, life's unpredictability,
life's painful beauty, a surgical use of sound

to remind us of all we can and can't be in this world,

in which there are so many, yet many are forever alone.

PASSION UNLIMITED UNLEASHED

The two astonishingly athletic men were
swept into the air by some stormy weather
conjured by a sweep of Cab Calloway's hand,

a mighty gesture lifting the Nicholas Brothers
into a wildly tapping dance, airborne more than not,
and musicians unleashed a ferocity of sound that

led the brothers to bound from table to table,
from floor to roof, bringing audiences to their feet;
oh, that building shook, rattled, and rolled in sympathy

with the flying feet, amazing splits, tap tappity tapping;
all in the room were hypnotized by the orchestra; horns
and drums unleashed the brothers in full flight; the mesmerizing

presence, lyrics, and mad joy of Cab Calloway led all present
into a beautiful chaotic land of sonic, kinetic, and visual delight.

HARRY IS CONFUSED

"As I age," Harry told Mortimer, his oldest

and only friend, "Sometimes things beyond
my ken, my ability to affect, make me weep:
a wee bairn sobbing while her parents scold
her, a dog being put to sleep, a dead bird
in a field, (one of its coal black wings flapping

in a cool breeze), a three year old slowly

succumbing to leukemia, married folk screaming
at one another for no apparent reason, two geezers
swinging weak punches at one another and falling
down from the exertion, arguments over nothing
with people who mean nothing to me, loss of all

belief in anything, whether this world or the next,

and my tears at such times confuse me; alcohol
does not relieve the unexplained grief; I have no
connection to these people or things; but I am
stricken by what I see. And my mind and heart
are lost upon a stormy sea that sweeps me

into personal doldrums where all is confusion."

BURROWING INTO SELF
(for Alma Peggy Newell)

In silence we find the heart, the soul,
the essence of who we are.
A bird soaring, a dolphin leaping above the sea,

a bear strolling through a wood, an owl floating
through the night are all at one
with self and surroundings.

Seated in an open field where a breeze caresses my neck,
I hear a mother call her children across road, stream,
and stand of trees, and her voice will echo for decades

while her children grow and flow across lands and time.
Listening, I discover a still center I did not know I have;
eyes close and I grow aware of one insect (which I had not noticed)

singing nearby, as my mother's voice sings from a well deep
within my mind. Breathing slows, and each hair on head and neck shivers.
A mist covers the land. I drowse and dream.

Kigali, Rwanda, Autumn 2012

WHO IS HE

Leafing through dozens
of old photos, I discover
a wide range of selves,
private selves, teacher selves,
athlete selves, theatre selves,

a lad, a man, an ancient,
bearded, clean shaven,
mustachioed, wearing
sideburns of all lengths
and shapes; the body

is thin, sturdy, portly,
obese, athletic, barely
functional, a person
who is scarcely recognizable
from one picture to the next;

none of these photos quite
match the face in the bathroom
mirror; something is wrong,
off-kilter; "it is the mirror's
fault," I murmur to self.

Which self do I address?
Do I know me well enough
to know to whom I speak?
It has become harder and harder
to find myself, to recognize

the other half of conversations;
I leaf again through all photos
accumulated over decades;
everyone I see is a stranger, as are
those who inhabit my mirrors.

I am left with the detritus
of time, places, and events,
yet nowhere is self evident
to me; I am a stranger in my own
body and mind, a relic without relative.

STILL-LIFE

An old fellow sat
on a bench by a river
free of human presence,
watching night's long awaited
arrival; his lips murmured words
of gratitude, his arms lifted in welcome,
and birds soared above headed westward.

A MISPLACED LAD

In school the bairn created a hullabaloo,
and teachers cajoled, scolded, roared
in attempts to gain his attention;

When alone in fen, forest, or moor,

or in a rowboat on a lake, he was silent
as a day without wind; he stalked
rabbits, deer, a wide assortment of birds,

was completely still even when fishing;

in class he was a noisy stranger;
outside class, he was an element
of the landscape as much as bush,

tree, creature, wind, or rain.

SAILING SOLO

An old man attired in ragged threads
stood bareheaded on a moor, his hair
flowing in the wind, his face tilted
up into the rain as though seeking
baptism, but the only gifts he could
find were remnants of a sinking sun

turning clouds deep purple that painted
his face with a beauty rarely seen in him
in his fading days that were slowly
vanishing as were sun and clouds,
and he sang a melancholy tune
only known to him, and he blessed the rain.

FOOLS ARE WE ALL

Lover, foolish lover, grasps love
from the wind, arms spread wide;
lofty sun and golden clouds elicit

hope for passion that will last and last;
beauty once seen, one wishes, will not vanish,
kind gestures will blossom, not wither,

and breezes in groves will sing of embrace,
and never turn to howls of rejection;
thus pray lovers, foolish lovers, young and old.

STILLED VOICES

Watching videos of musical artists from the fifties,

sixties, and seventies, I realize a majority
of the musicians I grew up on have died, and I am left
alone with recordings, but nothing new will be coming

from those who mattered most to me. Many of my

classmates from fifty and more years ago have also
moved on down the road. I am abandoned to face
the few years left, trying to find solace in memory,

but it fades, and I am seldom certain what is true,

and what is fiction that I concoct, in order to find
some joy, hope, meaning, connection, but even
my imagination has lost its potency, and I sit

and rock, sit and rock, and stare into a foggy night.

ALL THAT REMAINS IS A QUESTION

All fades away, all slips
into time's thickets, like
the final notes of a Miles Davis
solo drifting into foggy night.

I cannot remember names
of women I loved, of those
who have held me in their arms
as an act of passion and comfort.

I hear the waves of time coming
closer, as they prepare to carry me
past the barrier reef into the endless
sea which will sweep me into eternal darkness.

I have no belief, but I nonetheless hope,
and pray for a future of endless music, music, music.

CURSES AND BLESSINGS

As I stroll through city streets, I slowly realize
my clothes are too old, too ragged, too faded, yet
they serve me well, and have done so for many
years; some of the clothes have accompanied me
for decades. I slide along streets, alleys, and sidewalks

(often beyond repair), in shoes that have been my
companions in Bolivia, Rwanda, Oregon, and Florida,
wearing a tweed cap that I have owned in Uzbekistan,
Estonia, Mexico, Arizona, and Saudi Arabia, as well
as the other places listed above. The hat is battered,

twisted partially out of shape, faded, still
comfortable, and protective against the elements.
Certain books on my shelves have been there since
university days, read and reread, until the print is vague,
the covers have wandered off, and the places I acquired

the books long forgotten; yet the books, when I pick them
up, sing to me, and faces long faded whisper across the years,
in voices that summon many whom I am not certain I recognize.
Memory slides into the sea, and I hear the lost calling to me
from across the waves, "Remember, Remember, once

we knew and valued one another, once only our friendship
and the future mattered. I see shapes dancing in the distance,
but eyes have the gift of uncertainty which allows me to name
all I see, according to whims entirely personal, and my hearing
which has drifted away allows me to hear whatever I want.

DARING IS A FRAGILE THING

On certain days the winds of life lift me
like a branch in flight broken free from its tree
bringing the joy of being unaware of where one
is headed yet terrifying me with all the things
that might happen beyond my ability to discern
or control while creating dreams of a new life

whisper I to myself I have always wanted to rise
above all around me and discover new worlds
and the devil answers be safe avoid chances
return to your tree I will convince it to accept
you back to rejoin your lifelong community
I look down and discover flight has become terrifying

wonder intimidates and I settle to earth the tree
has already forgotten me and I must make do with
anything that is near to hand as I sink into the forest

JUST ANOTHER LATE AFTERNOON

Diminutive Dave,
of nine or ten years,
swiftly scampers
up and down stairs,
chasing neighborhood dogs and cats;

his mother's voice flings itself
off walls, steps, and through windows,
in furious pursuit,
doing its own wild,
parental tarantella, a step or two behind her untamed lad;

a large fellow appears at top of stairs,
and announces all will be still, and silence
will obtain;
as echoes of his voice
are swallowed by his large billowing beard,

a convergence of sizeable black birds
solemnly convenes on wires overhead;
the mother scans approaching clouds,
the bairn gathers himself as though
preparing to launch his missile of a body once again

swiftly in a childhood's wild uncontrollable dance, yet when lightning
scrawls its signature across heaven's vault
it unleashes an abandonment of thunder,
and all -- man, child, mother, and birds -- vanish;
the symphony of thunder and rain redefine landscape, as night,

stormy night, sweeps across a cityscape drained of all save wind and water.

NEVER FULLY KNOWN BUT ALWAYS SEARCHING

A rush of winds sweeps through
canyons that fill my heart and mind,
winds soaring with a lifetime of memories,
and I stare at what was long past,
but never forgotten, events and people
who still shape what I was and am;
they are beyond my reach, but I still twist
and turn in their grasp, never to find freedom
until I am no more; some of these people
and things have blessed me; some have
cursed me; and many have changed me
without my awareness; new events
and people sail through these canyons,
changing me once again, often unawares,
and I wander unknowing and unknown,
alone in my own dazed mind, a hobo of the heart.

A SYMPHONY OF MOVEMENT

Wildly whirling while backlit
by a fiery sunset, a woman invented
a loose-limbed dance, filled

with leaps, twirls, bends, and swirls,
as her long black hair unfurled

in rising and falling wind,
and I stopped some distance away
to witness and celebrate the woman's

ecstatic movement and marriage
with the elements, and allow all I saw

to become imprinted in my mind, to forever
remind me of how one person can both praise
and meld oneself to world's magnificence.

SWEPT INTO TIME'S DEPTHS

life's chords blend
as I approach my end
wind rain and fire rend
my bones as I descend
toward midnight
slip into a small craft
designed to carry me

over and beyond
Tennyson's bar
into time's great sea
where whatever may
or may not be waits
with indifference
to whatever sense I might

or might not make
of what is there
as I drift into my future
I hear a rising symphonic
summation of all I have
and have not done
as I am swept into time's depths.

MY WALKING STICK

carved from a madrone tree,
by a stranger I have never met,

balances me, accepts my considerable
weight, and permits me to lurch

around my neighborhood; albeit
gracelessly, nonetheless I can

reach destinations without tumbling,
stumbling, or otherwise embarrassing

this sack of old bones that I inhabit;
this sturdy stick has become my legs, arms,

feet, and stick shift to grant me speed, direction,
and conviction I can reach my destination.

NO CHAINS NO BOUNDARIES

Daddy hot lips, Mr. Calloway, scat sings round the stage,
and the Brothers Nicholas return bip for bop, dit for dat,
riddley foh fop for doodley do dop. The brothers need a cab,
but Calloway tells them to find their own musical journey;
and the two little men fly higher than seems possible. They

lift off, riding big band notes nearly out of sight, then fly
back to earth, slide into splits, then fly once again sky high.
Music lifts and lowers in perfect harmony with the Brothers'
feet and legs as they paint the stage with improbable, electrifying,
swirling movement, and the audience oohs, ahs, and beats their feet

in time to the dance. The band is joined to the brothers and Cab
Calloway's direction, and every audience member imagines being
able to fly, sing, and play instruments simultaneously, and never
need to take a breath, or return to earth. When movement ceases,
music fades into the atmosphere, the audience explodes into wild

cacophony of voice, slapped hands, and stomping feet. Life is renewed.

JERRY DOUGLAS

His dobro, whether singing and swinging
bluegrass, country, folk, Americana, Paul Simon,
Marcus Mumford, jazz gentle or rough and ready,

or Celtic from the heart of Ireland or Scotland, is always
blue all the time, all songs or tunes he plays break

a listener's heart, elicit tears, yet set feet to tapping
and bodies to bopping in their seats, create music
that recreates the rhythms of life that underlie all music,

whether air, tune, melody, jig, reel, strathspey, hornpipe,
march, ballad, or wild combination of unexpected

musical marriages that lead to sound landscapes never
before discovered, and the body and heart uncover
joy, grief, hope, loss, and beauty previously unknown.

WHERE AND WHEN AM I

the river is wide and I can't cross o'er
yet my mind sails across a thousand times
in search of the one woman I never forgot

she waves as I approach then disappears
and I find myself back on the bank
from where I first set sail

I mount clouds and float across
in the middle of a cloud flotilla
and awake to find myself again landlocked

ah wind water sky and cloud hold immense
beauty beauty such as my lost beloved emanates
yet I am forever lost as I search for her

daily the sun sinks behind mountains
and subsumes all I love know and seek
I sink into sleep mourning all I cannot reach

all night long the wind sings a melody of loss
in dream I murmur when will wind set me free
and I wake staring at loss across a mighty river

LAD WITH BOTTLENECK GUITAR

The lad waiting for English class to start
always played slide guitar, improvising
melodies and inventing lyrics about
hunting and fishing, lyrics he never
finished and which often veered into
descriptions of female classmates,
some of whom would dare him to sing
about them, challenge inevitably accepted.

I would suggest he put the guitar away, but
classmates would beg for one more song,
always one more, a process that would
never end unless I turned into an ogre,
which would prompt one final partial song,
a bluesy lament about teachers who lacked
heart, who lacked love of music, and a final
line lamenting my inability to dance.

FOR PATRICIA

I was listening in my apartment to Bach's
Brandenburg Concertos (with Heinz Holliger
playing oboe) while I corrected final exams.
At the time I was teaching in Tallinn. Somehow
a copy of Screen Actors' Guild Magazine
found its way into my hands. It was near the end
of a school semester, my workload nearly completed,
and I took a few minutes to skim the magazine.
I discovered a listing of actors who had died
in the previous year. I had only visited the states

a very few times in the previous twelve years,
yet discovered many names I recognized who
had departed. Halfway through the list of the deceased,
I found a name which shook me, which I had not thought
of for many years, a name of an old friend for whom
I once had great affection. We had worked on plays,
shared meals, attended operas, gone to see
one another's performances, visited one another's homes,
been as close as two people could be who were not
in love. We shared dreams, hopes, mistakes, weariness

at life's vicissitudes, and laughter, a great deal of laughter.
She had lived much of her life in Los Angeles,
where we had been something more than friends,
but less than lovers, Los Angeles which was 5600 miles
from where I sat in Estonia, reading of her unexpected
demise, unable to cry, unable to believe cancer could have
toppled someone a few years younger than myself. Later
I discovered she had died in Florida where she was apparently
working in professional theatre, having moved away from film
and television. I was reading of a stranger, but a stranger

who had been an important friend and colleague, whom
I directed in a theatre production, with whom I performed
in scenes for acting classes, who brought me down to Padua Hills
to see her work in fascinating plays written for a playwright's workshop.
To this day I keep expecting to hear from her, keep remembering
discussions, passionate yet civil disagreements, and find myself
cursing the cigarettes she never stopped smoking which
undoubtedly contributed to her cancer. I hate (and hated)
cigarettes, but I never stopped enjoying her company and her talent,
her formidable, daring, uninhibited talent. I sat there staring

into space after reading of her death, accompanied
by Bach's solemn beauty, while scenes from a life floated past.

BROTHER WHERE ARE YOU

From nearby apartment, horn half-soars,
half-staggers, and a voice battered by years

half-talks, half-sings, "Brother Where Are You
They Told Me That You Came This Way;"

and I recall Oscar Brown Junior singing this song
on a college stage fifty-four years ago;

even now as two old men revisit words and melody
with less than perfect command of voice and horn,

I am moved, and I see across the years Brown
and his amazing band electrifying the audience;

I bless the old men on a porch doing what they
can do to make the song live decades later.

Once again music has tied my declining years to a time
when all was hope, and life was defined by song.

SO MUCH IS UNFORESEEN

Two leaned against a rock wall,
a boulder looming overhead,
and held one another close,
as rain created a falling curtain;
a sheet of water dripped from rock
above as the couple became one

against a wet world that
enveloped them while nearby
a scramble of children dashed
through rain tossing flower pots
full of water at one another,
screaming when thunder growled,

pelting one another with bits of hail,
while the couple grew closer together
and imagined a future that never
came, a future that instead
shook them apart with a force
like lightning striking nearby trees.

Yet for an hour or so, the two were one,
two intertwined like roots of adjacent trees.

OUTSIDE MY MOTEL IN KIGALI

Mud on the road, mud is the road,
down into a valley of huts, tin buildings,
open air businesses of barter and exchange;
everyone knows everyone; all live
in brick, clay, or aluminum homes, one
or two rooms; people gather here, there,
everywhere there is open air space

to ramble and assemble, unfurl jive talk,
that ever-loving jive in your face,
eliciting laughter, cat calls, and now and again
a slip sliding jive step or three or four
in and out of doors; young women strut past,
brush off advances from assemblies
of smiling, laughing, exuberant young men;

elders rock in chairs while they remember
all they have seen and known, all who have
vanished in time's ancient river, time which seems
forever when young, and so fleeting when old,
time which has buried itself in their bones;
I wander past amused, amazed, agog, agape, joyful
that I still have a foot in this world which slowly

devours me, and all the old folk like me,
and all the laughing, dancing, chatting, beautiful
young men and women unaware soon they too
will take a place in a rocker on a porch;
and I hum to myself, "Hard times come again
no more no more no more," and I dream
of all that has been and all that might be.

(2011-2014)

AN OLD MAN'S PRAYER

A full moon sweeps across landscape outside
my home, ferrying a host of ghosts (from
a long life) which drift down a rising tide
to greet me one last time with the aplomb

reserved for those who have nothing to lose.
I, alas, still struggle to understand
how I can achieve things that will set loose
my guilt over failures, allow hope's expansion,

allow grief in a falling leaf to sift
into heart and mind, antidote to free
me from my catalogue of sins, a gift
granting peace in life, so I can let be.

Let me accept what was, is, shall be, face
loss, success, still embrace life's wild amazement.

ANDEAN TONE POEM

Music rises from the land, an upwelling,
swelling of the earth, the birth of mountains,
the stirring of wind, the twisting, thrusting,
rearing, heaving aloft of stone, dirt, and tree,

the jutting peak, the infolding of self, the unfolding
of plain, the carving of canyon, the harsh, rocky
faces crossing centuries above which generations
of birds soar. This vast chorus humbles man

and exalts all that is inhuman, unnameable,
not malleable, all that is beyond human control
or knowledge, all that strives for the unknown,
the unknowable, the vaulting sky, all we (you

and you and you and I friends) can never know
or be or aspire to, all that rises above man's ken.

La Paz, Bolivia, December 2008

HE WHO DREAMS A LIFE

No one knows my heart who does
not love the night filled with silvery
moon, glittering star, streaking comet, and,
above stands of trees, an owl ghosting.

No one knows my midnight mind who does
not see, hear, or feel wind, rain, mountain,
stream, river, and ocean populating
the dreams which flow from night into day.

No one knows me who has listened
to tales of distant plateaus, dolphin and whale,
wolf and bear, stately redwood and fir stretching
to the horizon, and not imagined a life of travel.

No one can understand, whose heart is entwined in
the daily minutiae of the life of man, why I am as I am .

La Paz, Bolivia (October 24, 2008)

SIX IN THE MORNING

Almost every morning in La Paz,
I peered through an apartment window,

staring toward cloud-capped, sun-laced
mountains soaring in the distance,
an occasional bird drifting through clouds,

and I would quietly sing, "Hard Times Come
Again No More," as I watched Aymara

Indians walk down mountain roads from uptown,
and from El Alto, to the homes and businesses
who employed them at far less than American

minimum wages, amazed at how true
the lyrics of Stephen Foster's song was,

both for the Aymara and for many Americans;
from more than a century ago, Foster's words
were prescient and cut to the bone.

The beauty of the landscape was breathtaking;
the lives lived by so many were heartbreaking.

ALWAY THERE IS MUSIC

A wanderer, a gambler, a wild heart
who rambles up and down hills,
across valleys, he loves to drum

the land he crosses with his feet
beating out a heartbeat, at times
slow, other times rapid, but always

a beat beat beat that suggests
he bestows life through his feet
as he wanders thither, hither, round

and about, and always he sings
old songs he has known for decades;
he breathes music, he converses

through tunes, rhyme, and rhythm,
he defines life through music he hears,
shares, creates, repeats; he walks

with a lilt and bounce to his step; his
voice, singing, humming, speaking,
or whispering, always seems at one

with breeze, wind, falling water,
or thundering sky; all life, he says,
is music, and all music enriches life;

even when he snores while sleeping,
he sounds as though he were some old
singer such as Louis Armstrong, Clark Terry,

or even perhaps Son House or Howling Wolf;
the world entire is a cauldron bubbling music
music music; without it life is bereft.

A FINAL SONG'S EMBRACE

Sing a song full and free, born from childhood,
as we race through damp spring fields;
listen to choirs of birds
rejoice in lands without rules,
and these hours and days
find homes that last for years on end;
yet eventually slip away, arm in arm with me,
as time redefines and sends me across life's
final bar, where I will slip into final embrace
of existence and learn who I am.

A FEW FINAL WORDS

Perpend
old friend
we soon
must blend
with our end

everlasting darkness
glides ever closer
brings our tryst with naught
into view our sexual congress
with nothingness

forgive me oh lord
I bring no thing to share
with whatever may exist
beyond this dying world
not even a solitary useful word

I slip from here to there
in quiet grief that I am
alone and unable to be useful
I wonder will whispers follow me
he was only a fool a fool a fool

THE ANCIENT

The ancient crumpled on the park bench
had a face resembling a shelf of second hand
books, musty and unopened for years.
His voice, tattered, whiskey-soaked, muttered
fragments of half-forgotten poems, and snippets
of song lyrics twisted out of shape. Passersby

took circular routes around him. Even pigeons
avoided strutting in his direction. From time
to time, he would stare at something happening
in other areas of the park and rasp a laugh
before resuming his recital of scraps of poems
and songs. A drunk emerged from a stand of trees,

ensconced himself on the old man's bench.
Without even looking at him, the drunk passed
him a bottle of cheap rum. The ancient
took a swig and began to recite Falstaff's speech
about honor. The drunk reclaimed his bottle
and wandered off, bestowing a flip of his hand

as a goodbye. The old man slowly sank
into what looked like a pile of dirty laundry.
No one approached. As dusk arrived,
the old fellow began to snore in ragged
strips of sound, punctuated by loud snorts.
Night claimed park and old man. All were invisible.

JOURNEYS

Kigali's dirt roads
have their own logic,

as do the journeys
of children and the wise;

often a twist or turn
returns a traveler

to the beginning
but with fresh perspective.

TUTORIAL

A girl chatted with a grove
of trees, listened to whispers
from a flower garden and replied.

This made me chuckle,
this discourse with
growing things;

yet older now I nod my head
at crows, greet songbirds
with familiarity, embrace

wind, wave at the moon, sing
and dance with pouring rain,
maintain sacramental silence

passing heron frozen in solemn
stillness. All things seen
and heard expand who I am.

WE CALLED HER DAISY

(for Malgosia Turzanska)

The girl spoke to flowers, bushes, plants, trees,
bees, and other creatures that enrich the earth,
and who is to say she was wrong, as creations
of beauty flowed from her mind, heart, fingers,

and unlimited imagination. She birthed drawings,
paintings, poems, stories, and wild journals in which
she explored all manner of creatures, ideas, hopes,
delights, possibilities. and unnameable landscapes.

We, who found amusement in the idea of talking
to plant life and animals, were astonished by worlds
she could summon through pen, pencil, or paint brush.
Such connection to the world is easily mocked; less

easily explained is how such perception opens up
the world and unleashes beauty, beauty, beauty.

WE DON'T KNOW EACH OTHER

The bearded man on the bicycle rides
all over this damned town that time forgot
(or perhaps never knew); he is stocky,

with wild gray hair, and a balding path
down the center of his scalp; his beard
is grizzled, with wild patches of brown
and white. We don't know each other,

but we know each other as travelers
of all the roads in town, he on his
clunky bike, and I a pedestrian
with a walking stick carved from a branch;

we always salute one another solemnly,
then smile, but never speak; if we
run into one another in a store,
we nod and go about our business;

we don't know each other, but we know
each other, fellow wanderers, solo
and happy in the rain, the sun, the wind,
the brilliance of day, and the sprawl
against the evening sky of the gloaming;

we are free from car, cell phone, calendar,
obligations of family, business,
church, and community; we are ghosts

visible only to one another as we pass
back and forth from one side of town
to another, pursuing our peculiar fancies;

we are de-flocked birds, or wandering
herd animals who have lost contact
with our kin; our passing, frequent

or infrequent, always provokes a smile,
two old men who grin in recognition
and pass by without need for speech.

WHO WOULDA THUNK IT

She was not
beautiful, not even
by generous standards:

her nose was too large;
her eyes, while remarkable
for their brown depths,

looked in different directions,
as though seeking answers
everywhere at once;

her mouth was a river
with multiple bends
in its path;

and her chin resembled an aging,
forgotten pier waiting for cargo
long overdue to arrive and be unloaded;

yet when she grinned,
onlookers broke into
wide smiles;

and when she laughed, people
sang and danced
in ecstatic celebration;

her homely face when joyful
was a unique definition
of symmetry and beauty

that freed all in her presence from
glum every day worries, transmuted
the aching quotidian into fiesta.

AND SO IT GOES AND GOES AND GOES

Cracked leaf, cracked heart,
where does love start?

Spring breeze, spring song,
whisper love dusk to dawn.

Shattered leaf cannot be healed;
cracked heart at times
may be annealed.

As one ages, one discovers
full-throated song
bestows recovery.

Over time one will learn
there is no love that's
not been earned.

MUSIC ABOUNDS

Trees throughout a village
are in intimate conversation
with wind and one another;

pine and palm vary between
whispers and operatic arias,
and an old man leans against

a wall and eavesdrops on such
wild, uninhibited expression
of self, and wishes he were

young again and unafraid
to sing full-throated while
inventing song and dance

that fills a day with delight,
and serenades night's dimming
of the day as all fades away.

MUSIC IS EVER PRESENT

solitary songbird
                hidden
in bushes
        along creek bank
bursts into song
                as ancient chap strolls past

he stands still on his path
        enchanted by the piping of birdsong
the notes could be Herbie Mann improvising
                or thoughts surprising thoughts
dancing in cool morning air
        or notes of a hammered dulcimer in exuberant flight

the bird drifts into silence
        and the old fellow moves on humming softly to self
                and wind licks at leaf and bush
        while lad on nearby pier drums on soaked boards

BUMBLING HITHER AND THITHER

Wind blows, and branches
bow, sway, hurl themselves
this side and that, and my hat

unmoors itself, races down
the street, over bush, betwixt
buildings, through parking lots,

and lands on top of a closed
rubbish bin, where I (panting
profusely) spear it with my walking

stick amidst a storm of curses, snarls,
and threats to its well-being, as I lean
against the bin, chagrined at my

physical limitations, replace hat upon
head, and slowly galumph toward home.

MANY DREAMS CANNOT BE ABANDONED

Ah, the music of motion through the air:
gymnasts twirl, spin, soar, flip, fly,
redefine earth and sky; dancers lift off
into space with an elegance and grace

beyond definition; certain athletes (high
jumpers, long jumpers, pole vaulters,
basketball players, to name a few)
renew our belief in flight as beauty's

essence; lads and lasses discover
their bodies in games, dances, and dreams
of youth, dreams that reoccur long after
our bodies have abandoned our wild,

imaginative fantasies of wonder, unrestrained
movement, hope for all that can be named
or fathomed, even in the least degree. All
movement is music, designed to flow with music,

and all imagination flows from night music of the mind.
There is a powerful reason that many prayers are sung.
Prose is too often pedestrian. Poetry is musical language.
Music is poetry released on bird wings in expansive flight.

ARE SOME SONGS TOO CLUMSY FOR UTTERANCE

A lad blows mightily upon his trumpet;
cracked notes empty the living room
he claims for his concert hall. One brother
remains to sing along, his voice slipping

into cracks between notes, and the family hound
howls in sympathy, a sound mighty, yet
unmusical. A cat stalks out a window,
in high dudgeon, refusing to move swiftly,

but each step utters contempt, contempt,
utter contempt. The three remaining, neophyte
trumpeter, inept singer, and canine accompanist,
are unaware of others' despair at their concert.

The joy felt in their wondrous freeform dissonance
unleashes a freedom enriching chaotic explorations.

OUT FOR A STROLL

Late afternoon sunshine
and a cool breeze inform
my aged stride, infusing it
with a bounce long forgotten,
giving my gait a lopsided grin.

A BAIRN'S MIND ADRIFT

A lad lifts his eyes high,
high above in pursuit
of his greatest love,

the midnight sky,
alive with stars, moon,
drifting clouds, and dark

emptiness, which encompasses
all he sees and cannot see,
loves yet cannot know,

and his mind soars,
but is landlocked, and all
he sees and cannot see

will fill his dreams
when finally he pulls his head
back into his room to sleep

and free his mind into infinite
floating drifting search
for all he will never know,

that will always whisper
his name night and day,
awake or asleep,

a smile upon his lips.

ON A WINTRY AFTERNOON

palm and pine sing
in the wind
and dark clouds
scud cross the sky
I lift my face
to blustery wind

and it blends
with rain flung from
horizon to horizon
my glasses awash
in windblown water
I lean against a wall

so as not to fall
and laugh with neighbor
who stands in his door
face to the rain
two old men lost
in the elements

with no sense of time
or place but adrift
in late afternoon storm
out of place but at peace
with wind water
and oncoming night.

I REMEMBER EVERYTHING
(variations on an idea of John Prine)

I recollect honeysuckle under starlight, hide
and go seek under moonlight filtered through
flotillas of clouds, fireflies captured in jars,
blackberries picked during chilly autumn
evenings -- one for the jar, two for the mouth,
two for the jar, one for your partner
in theft, parents' voices echoing off hills,
increased urgency of summons dragging us
homeward ever faster, ever more reluctantly,
often reaching home just as rain showers began,

and dinner was served; yet meal and rain
did not change the desire to return to the magical
world of darkness filled with flitting shapes
of children, moon and stars sailing through
cloudscapes, and the mysterious presence of owls
floating above; parents say, "Tomorrow,
tomorrow will come soon enough and the night
will once again welcome you into its embrace."
Falling into sleep, I hear a nearby creek's burble,
and I float downstream in dreams all through the night.

CHIMES OF NIGHT

A great horned owl soars above silent forest,
its fluted whisper leaves a listener breathless.

A golden moon, in full sail through scattered clouds,
spills waves of light upon silent, darkened homes,

its serenity a visual version of Bach played
on the oboe by Heinz Holliger.

In a darkened midnight window, an elderly widow
hums in her broken voice the Handel Sarabande in D Minor,

and wonders how such music could have once been banned.
A distant train rumbles past; rising wind sweeps sky free of clouds.

PASSAGE OF A HEART

Wind bends columns of snow
into serpents weaving
through heavy air;

on a deep fall night,
stars are strewn like leaves
across an unraked yard;

a many voiced litany
of waves sprawls
knees-first onto a nearby beach;

such moments compose
the passage
of a heart,

as does a gecko on a wall
hanging near the ceiling
in patient suspense;

and consider an old fellow
who swims robustly through
a deep river of memories.

Ah, the heart, the heart, whose songs
never cease, whether lyric or mournful,
your embrace permits and defines meaning.

UNEXPECTED TURNS OF FORTUNE

There is a sense of familiarity
that comes with rediscovering
a poem one has previously enjoyed

and then forgotten. Rather like
being offered a tasty cupcake
or square of fudge unexpectedly,

and, to one's surprise, discovering
one has encountered this treat previously,
and, lo and behold, it is even more

delectable, more of a treat
than one remembers. Second
discoveries of old lovers do not

seem to turn out this way, but
sometimes she (or he) is the one
offering the brownie or fudge square,

so all, for the time being, is forgiven.
At least now you have found that you share
something that leaves you both smiling.

WHAT NEXT

She faded into couch cushions,
suddenly a child at ninety-four,
when without warning her brain retuned
and words made sense that from her poured.

These reversals came and went. No one
knew from hour to hour whether
sense or nonsense from her lips would run;
there was no predicting her mind's weather.

The grief that came, when she turned child, became
fear when lucidity reappeared,
fear clarity would swiftly disappear,
leaving all uncertain whether grief or shame

was what they felt, grief at bludgeoning loss,
or shame their words and cures were dross.

WINDBLOWN

Lifted and launched by wild April wind:
trees, leaves, bushes, stray dogs, feral cats,
coveys of bairns, and my wandering self
who ends up on streets never before visited,
discovers parts of a river previously only seen

from a distance, while in sky above an armada
of cumulus clouds piled high like bales of cotton
stream past like freighters I once saw float
down the Rhine River on a spring afternoon in Dusseldorf
as brisk as this day tilting my small town upside down.

ALL ARE CAUGHT IN THE END

Lads race up and downhill through tall stands of grass,
While old men sip beer, cheer what once they did.
Youth may be served, but, alas, time must pass.
Lads race up and downhill through tall stands of grass,
Their legs moving swift as wind until time grasps
Flesh, renders a clumsy image of what once sped.
Lads race up and downhill through tall stands of grass,
While old men sip beer, cheer what once they did.

CAUGHT BY SURPRISE

On certain days the wind celebrates your beauty,
lifts your hair, waves it for all to see, and sings
its praises, as men turn to watch your passing,
stunned by beauty unaware of itself, and women
stare in surprise that such loveliness can float past

and not proclaim itself, but simply exist in harmony
with tree, bush, gently undulating branch,
while birds swirl overhead as though painting
a mighty canvas that can never be overburdened,
and at last you disappear, and all shake themselves
as though waking to the day, and setting off astonished
on a new, thoroughly unexpected, unknown journey.

AN OLD MAN CELEBRATES HIS COMPANION

Your hair adrift in a spring breeze
carries me back through decades, waves
as you jog forest paths, ages, changes
color from auburn to grey over years,
as time has us both in its grasp, re-coloring
hair, filling joints with arthritis, mutating

the way we once soared together into
gimpy limping relics of another time, and yet,
and yet, and yet, behind those lines,
I see even today the wild grin of youth,
the exuberant laughter that came unbidden
and was inexhaustible, the gracious

smile and caress that forgave all and turned
difficult times into sagas of hope, and no,
you have never abandoned our journey
together no matter how often we slipped and fell,
and for all these things and many more than I can
enumerate, I sing a song of love and possibility.

A TESTAMENT

An old man wrote and wrote and wrote.
How else could he justify a life where
fewer and fewer knew who he was,
what he had or had not done, could
recall defeats and triumphs celebrated
or mourned? The world grew larger
and larger, and he grew smaller, smaller,

ever smaller, as he became invisible
to a world speeding faster and faster past
his frozen in place home. So his fingers
danced upon a keyboard tracing a life
faded everywhere but in his mind. He
realized his memories could be wrong.
No one was left to share alternative

renderings of deeds done and undone.
Only his more and more faulty memory
could be relied on, and even in its best
days, it had been unreliable. He created
a dream of the past which may or may not
have been true, but at least it was testament
to a life, good or bad, outstanding, mediocre,

or worthless. The document was a slender
reed in the wind of time. It meant nothing
save to him. It was a hoarse, muted whisper
in time's hurricane that swept all before it.
The old man swore to write until he vanished,
aware few would read what he wrote, and even
fewer would care about his aged prattle.

Ah, the wind and rain and how we survive.

HIS HORN IN PURSUIT

trip slip bang head on floor
once more into fray
he may be drunk
but jazz can found everywhere
so he dives back into life
without fear of failure
his horn searches for truth
he ignores his clunkers
a moment of beauty here

or there forgives all
and each lures him back
into life's arms no matter
how poorly most of his music
is played one pure moment
of love an interlude
of wild laughter
tears' compassion
discovery of a friend

all his shortcomings are
forgiven for a time
however brief his successes
all is worthwhile as life's music
transmutes dross into gold
and his horn wanders
in perpetual pursuit
of beauty joy chaos reforming
into clarity and peace

sing brother sing

ON A WINTER EVENING

Storm swirls through pine and palm;
trees turn into wind-organs;
birds chart wild patterns
through evening skies; then
a cloudburst sweeps day away,

and all is darkness;
an old man sits in a doorway
baptized by gusts of rain,
face lifted with expectant joy
toward the exuberant heavens.

His acceptance of what is
brings song to his lips, cracked
baritone flung skyward
without apology, with desire
to merge with the elements.

REQUIEM FOR A MOTHER

Your ashes dispersed upon ocean waves;
your voice silent, yet I hear your lament
for your late husband, and I recall your

gentle loving touch of plants, trees,
dying friends, and your children, even
as time stretched you further and further

apart from all that once mattered to you.
I come across a picture of you lying in grass
as a student decades ago, and you are smiling

across the years. I realize I have never seen
you smile in a picture before. In this picture
all is before you, and life has not crippled you

or convinced you to expect nothing. All was
possible, and nothing was impenetrable.

APPROACHING MIDNIGHT

Night deepens, and wind extends
its reach from one side
to other of the sky.

Clouds scoot into,
then out of, sight
while full moon sails

through scattering and
reforming clouds, and trees
wave branches with wild

abandon, shedding twigs,
leaves, and sending shadows
scudding across dim lawns.

Wandering through neighborhood
without purpose, I find myself
singing, "I'm a man you don't meet

every day." An old woman on nearby
balcony shakes her head and goes inside.
Unrecalcitrant, I sketch a semblance

of a jig, and continue on my way,
now singing, "I've been a wild rover,"
waving my walking stick at the sky.

Bless the moon, bless the wind, bless
the wildly free clouds, and may they
welcome me into their brotherhood.

CONFABULATION

As I age, all memory and meaning
are confabulation, a bending of time,
place, action, and memory to a world
created to suit what I want things

to have been, to be, a willing of the world
I have dreamed to exist as I wanted it, not as
it in truth was; life as I recall it is less history,
and more a dream, or a fairy tale, or a richly

conceived fiction that is better suited
for an anthology of tales meant to please
wee bairns whose parents read them wildly
imaginative possibilities, not what is true;

I try to construe what is true, old or new,
but always my mind sails on uncontrolled journeys.

ALL IS ONE

Like distant waves,
leaves sang an evening
lullaby, welcoming
the gloaming's arrival;

the wind rose and fell,
cast a musical spell
throughout a sprawling
ancient dell, where owls

ghosted beneath a moon,
forest creatures quietly
sought shelter, an old couple
silently rocked, hands locked,

and a soft whisper of light rain
created midnight chamber music.

AN ACQUIRED TASTE

The old fellow in the diner
claimed his beer made
the world more clear.

The gimpy waitress laid
his meal down with a leer,
claimed his stew would be an escapade

in leftover scraps that would need the beer
to wash down the muck for which he'd paid.
The only thing worse than the meal was their frozen glare.

The food was so bad that cops turned down free meals.
Escaping without eating was the best available deal.
Even the apple pie made a grown man squeal.

A MINOR INCIDENT

Lad by pond catches fish,
proclaims it rainbow colored,
waves it at passersby in dusk,

walks home, pole over one shoulder,
fish over other, lilt in his stride,
singing, "I'm a man you don't

meet every day." I move slowly
in opposite direction humming
riffs on his melody, all the way home.

AN AFTERNOON ALONE WITH THE WEATHER

Wind blends with rain all afternoon;

the sky is evening by noon,
and I croon out of tune with old

Nat King Cole and Bing Crosby songs
in a voice badly worn by time,
yet exuberant in accompanying music

from childhood, unleashing joy,

grateful to be alone, so I feel free
to unleash remnants of a voice

ragged as old trousers worn too long;
I eventually laugh at how ludicrous
this all would appear to a stranger,

and I create a drumbeat of laughter

that unleashes my feet in a clumsy
stutter step homemade dance; and rain

strokes window panes like drum brushes,
with an unexpected grace that makes
me whirl and lean out the window

to accept water's blessing on face and shoulders.

PASSING THE TIME

He is alone, a stone
looming at his window.

He is not lonely, the wind again
and again visits and knows his name.

When storm clouds swirl above and thunder shakes
the neighborhood, he grins, roars with laughter.

Streets soaked with sheets of water, puddles dance,
as tires rollick past throwing pillows of water high above.

When storm is past, he plays slow movement from Beethoven's
7th Symphony, sits, cocks his head, turns stone who deeply hums.

A FEW MINUTES IN A LATE AFTERNOON

Barelegged in cool rain,
she strides freely downhill,
legs caressed by tall meadow

grass, head thrown back, hair
flowing in steady breeze
with grace of swan breasting

lake, and the solitary witness,
an old woman, crouched
beneath an oak tree, smiles,

and softly claps her hands, as
the young woman claims the world
through which she passes.

Rain, wind, setting sun bless,
for these few minutes,
young woman and old witness.

AVE TO THE STORM

All night snow whispered across
lawn, bush, tree, meadow,
and forest climbing side of mountains;

dawn brought a gale that set the world
a-tumble, tossed, turned, churned,
and the rumble, grumble, untidy roaring

that splintered trees, threw branches
throughout the neighborhood, unleashed
a volume of chaotic sound that rivaled

Beethoven's final symphonic movement,
a closing statement on life that sobs and prays
for one and all, and ends with a psalm

for whatever is still to come -- no complaint,
simply a full-throated howl for life, its loss,
its beauty, a prayer for one and all.

AS I STAND IN MY DOORWAY

wild wind song
        through cedar and palm
    brings rush of sleet

Beethoven's ghost is loose
        in swelling eventide
    feral music sweeps through the land

I slip inside
        seek a light switch
    I am still in darkness

night swallows all

LISTENING TO BEETHOVEN'S NINTH SYMPHONY

Thunder reverberates throughout La Paz.
In sympathetic vibration, the Andes respond.

I turn sixty-three and hear voices
murmuring across the years. Old fears and new

are summoned by the night, the future shrinks,
the past dims, and the moment expands

and diminishes as thunder rises and fades.
All these years and still there are no words

to describe what has been, what is, and what
is to come. The music ends,

as does the storm. Once again I am alone.
Still there is no peace, only the faint melody

of voices past and to come, the quiet
drumming of the heart, and a breeze

lifting and releasing living room curtains.
When rain brushes the window,

I set sail on an ocean of sleep.
Who knows where I will awaken?

(La Paz, Bolivia, October 31, 2008)

POET'S PRAYER

(listening to Beethoven's Ninth Symphony)

to follow a path anywhere it winds,
to feel wind loosen desire, never to tire
riding night, all its might surging

before a final swoop into the depths
of dream, a dazzling drop:

all song ceases, ceases all sound, sound
deceased and feet walk the earth once more (breeze
brushing sand) and my hands know once more
your face your face your face

WORDS WORDS WORDS

A casual stream of words among friends
flows with ripple, twist, and changing speed

of water through a mountain creek,
with mutating energy of a breeze

inciting branch, bush, and leaf to dance,
with astonishing shifts found in Andean weather

where rain, thunder, and sunshine follow
one another without rhyme or apparent reason,

as do verbal thrusts and parries of those
who know one another intimately,

generously, and fearlessly. These freeform
conversations, these riffs of wit, these hummingbird

flights of fancy, these verbal tangos, these oral
pas de deux are no more important than death,

the words no more serious than seeds distributed
in an open fertile field which has no owner.

Talk about weather or sports or politics
is never just about weather, sports, or politics.

It is the music of the heart, the dance
of intellect, soul, and unself-conscious passion,

an improvisation sketching all one is,
a self-portrait painted on the spot.

UNKNOWABLE

On my refrigerator hang pictures of my parents,
early twenties, faces fresh, alert, hopeful.

What were their dreams, how many
of those dreams have been realized?

What disappointments have remained cloaked?
What fears lurk beneath the parchment of their faces,

sixty or more years past the snapping of those photos?
These are things shrouded in mystery for their children.

Walking the bland streets of my compound in Riyadh,
the wind whispers their names. Children learning to ride bicyles

(parents trotting alongside) recall one or the other of my parents
running beside myself or a sibling, encouraging us to speed away.

A girl in the library puzzles over the words in a magazine;
her coaxing mother at her side summons a ghost from my past

who leads my path through flash cards into books and off
into a world of imagination and dream from which I have

never fully emerged. What were her dreams as I drifted away?
I write a lonely letter home from the Philippines, a young man confused

and full of teenage angst. My father's quiet words of comfort
string hope across the ocean between us.

I never answered, never formed those difficult words--thank you.
Did this teenage slighting of his gift carve lines into face and soul?

All night the wind humming through cracked windows has raised
questions, unleashed ghosts throughout the living room.

I try to sleep, but the mind lurks in ambush:
Do we ever really know our parents? Do we, do we, do we?

A SUMMONS

There was a neighborhood
through which I strolled
during many evenings
on the cusp of the gloaming.

In the middle of the walk,
I would come upon a graveyard,
stone-capped like spindrift
draping waves sweeping toward a beach.

On many evenings, crepuscule's deepening
purple made the gravestones appear to be
spilling blood, as though the landscape were
being painted with ichor, centuries of blood

uniting the fallen. When the wind whispered
through trees, I imagined I was being summoned.
I heard songs rising from a nearby creek, inviting
me to sink into earth, and feed bush, tree, and plant.

As I age, the summons grows stronger, the pull
more urgent, and I often feel like dancing into
the arms of every cemetery I stroll or drive past.
And yet I also want to sing as I sink into landscape.

REMEMBERING
(for Pungo)

I still feel his frail bones, hear his kind words, remember
(as we parted) his loving, spectral touch, my silence.
On my refrigerator is a picture of him and my mother,

smiling into the future and the raising of family,
faces unlined, no gray in hair, a fearless acceptance
in eyes for what might come. My mind adjusts,

recalls boyhood and the two people in the photo,
decades wiped away, the long journey just begun
which would end in a trailer with him in great pain

held in my mother's and brother's arms, while I returned
to a job as a surrogate parent for rich people's children
in a foreign land. I would seek forgiveness, if I knew

from whom and for what. When I look at the photo,
I hear whispers whose words I can not quite distinguish.
I imagine movement and think someone is about to walk

into the picture, a brother, a sister, me, and realize
I am still alone, still silent, still draped in confusion,
unable to reach through time, and seek a blessing.

AN EVENING RAMBLE

I stroll through autumn fields
replete with shattered leaves,
as dead grass waves in wind.
All all foretells my end.

Sun hastens to descend;
bleeding sky summons grief:
not for my end foretold,
nor for my days grown cold,

but for all I'll never know
of man, beast, plant, mountain, stream,
majestic sea's ebb and flow --
all fades into a dim dream.

Each step leads to a tomorrow
where no more days are left to borrow.

MEMORY TRANSFUSIONS

Whatever frisks, flocks, flies, or frolics
(bird, sheep, child, goat, chimp, porpoise,
bear cub, or whale), lifts the spirits

of all who watch and remember
when illimitable energy illuminated
the day and much of the night,

when sleep seemed a whim,
and even casual conversation
or a walk across campus or

a few city blocks could fill
the mind and body with excitement
and make the world's colors

exceed anything found on film
or canvas and turn the world's
sounds into music full of

fascinating nooks and crannies,
crescendos and decrescendos,
and climaxes never ending;

for those whose hearing, sight,
and energy have diminished, joy
exists in witness of whatever

found in the world unleashes
the tides of memory and infuses
day and night with cherished

recollection of what is forever lost
to time, forever present in thought,
imagination, and irrepressible hope.

LOST IN THE STARS

Tired of sitting, reading, listening to music,
contemplating my limitations and errors of judgement,

I struggle to my feet and go outside into a night
which startles me -- the air is brisker, the wind

blows with more vigor, and the night is darker
than I have anticipated. The moon is absent,

and the occasional people passing by are shapes
without faces, the goats are more sound than shape,

and the chickens are searching for places to shelter,
but the deep deep sky holds swarms of stars,

bright, faint, clear, dim behind a passing
cloud curtain, and I am drawn outside the dwelling

of my mind to a world I too often forget.
I stand motionless on a dirt road without lights,

feel a cool wind wrap itself around me, hear
a ragged impassioned choir in the distance, and

feel the long day (the sweat and grit of thought
and the struggle with imagination's limitations),

stripped from body and mind, as my breathing
slows, my vision stretches overhead to its limit,

and I rediscover my love for darkness, for starlight,
for a cool wind stirring the landscape around me,

and for the elegance of stillness in the midst
of passing life in its multitude of forms.

I stand speechless, devoid of thought, at peace
(a rare and blessed span of seconds or minutes

or more--I am not sure) until a friend approaches
to ask if I am alright. Startled, I stare, smile,

break into laughter, and realize I have offended
someone who is concerned for me. I try

to explain. He does not understand, but smiles
as though I have reassured him. I realize we don't

share enough language to deal with the nuances
of what I have just experienced, but since I seem

happy now, he is reassured that the crazy old man
is no threat to himself or anyone else. I return

to my room, but my mind (still, yet soaring,
full, yet emptied of thought) is lost in the stars.

Kigali, Rwanda, March 2013

HOIST SAIL

Rain's whisper fills the night.
I sit on a porch in another foreign country,

hear distant voices murmur in cadences
of French and Kinyarwanda and discover anew

the beauty of the strange, the different, the unknown.
I glance at the glass door behind me; reflected there

is yet another stranger, unknown after nearly sixty-six years.
All life is a question, no matter where I look.

Who, when all is said and done, are we?
I slip into sleep, my mind sailing the rain and my past.

Kigali, Rwanda, September 2011

THE PACKRAT

No never no never no
never again cried the bent man to the wind--
never again will I dance to the fiddle
that filled my spring days with leaps, shouts, and laughter;

my back crooks, a question mark
shaped like life, my fumbling life
that stumbles through alleys, down piers,
beneath rotting bridges where children's voices
peal out: look at the funny fat gray bearded man
tripping over his bellbottoms, his seedy old bellbottoms;

I pass lovers, my hungry eyes averted from their shrinking;
I pass lovers, my ears keen for every sound of passion,
scraps to feed on as darkness falls, as I creep under bushes
or trash bins, as my voice fondles swatches of melody
from boyhood, when the wind sang of flight into perpetual sun
and the moon and stars were a gem-studded shawl;

I pass lovers and stuff the pockets of my heart
with others' dreams to be sorted through greedily--
I know somewhere in these volumes I cart about
is a life I might have lived;
now even fresh fallen snow blackens beneath my swollen feet
wrapped in rags discarded by the profligate young;

to see only others, or the past, is my motto
as I huddle in the undemanding company of broken bottles,
tin cans, and the mind's ashes…

THE OLD CATCHER'S MITT

sits on a shelf, forgotten save when I open
the closet, and feel my aching knees complain
of hours spent crouched behind home plate
where I had no thought of any consequence
other than winning or losing;

sun spills through a half-opened window, bringing
voices of lads in an open field playing three flies up,
the smell of spring blossoms and new mown grass,
decades-old cries of a crowd, and the chatter of an infield
and those relegated to dugouts while I crouched

behind home plate signaling pitches,
gesturing fielders left or right, in or out,
often trying to convince an ump a bad pitch
caught the corner; a door opens and closes
nearby, and the spell is broken. The mitt is simply

old leather overdue for the trash, a repository
of nothing but juvenile memory. It is never to be
used again, and I reach to toss it into a rubbish bin,
but its ancient smell and feel stops me, tears form,
and I am not certain for whom or what I cry,

only that the mitt will survive this visit to the closet,
and I walk gingerly away on aching knees
with joys of the past and faces long forgotten
populating my thoughts, and a sad smile engraved
on the mask I wear to greet today's indifferent world.

TRANSFIXED

Night's mighty cathedral once again encompasses
my world, whirls my mind over city lights,
over mountains, into a vast starscape, an expanse
beyond language's ability to describe. I am

lost in an epic sky, lost in the universe I once
inhabited as a boy, as a dreamer, as a weaver
of tales known only to myself and a friend or two.

Now I recite no tales, I imagine nothing, I dream nothing,
I merely stare and wonder what imagination designed

the cold immense beauty which pierces my heart and mind.

La Paz, Bolivia (May 2010)

A CELEBRATION

This is a day to pick blackberries,
to taste honeysuckle and bathe
in its fragrance, to be breeze-blown
across town to parks where children
romp across fields and climb trees,
to take off hats and feel sun and wind
on face and through hair, this is a day
to dare imagining that life is full
of unexpected and intoxicating pleasures.

A CELEBRATION?

Stone, stone, alone in a field,
whistles solitary tune in winter wind;

tree, tree, one, two, three, swirl in breeze, dance,
prance, bow, scrape, snap upright;

these bones, old bones, which I wearily
inhabit, shake, rattle, and moan throughout

my clumsy traipse through fields, woods,
past creek, pond, and river; and I sing

with the wind, caw with crows, honk
at passing geese, release all fears into

dark clouds rushing in my direction,
bearing rain, lightning, and the roar of thunder.

A child's voice shouts, "Hey, Mister, are you crazy?"
I bellow back, "Almost certainly. Damn, it feels good."

DELIGHT CAN BE FOUND UNEXPECTEDLY

As the gloaming settles upon
a town, night breathes, silence
envelops house, yard, street,

bush, and tree, and one leaf
loses its grip and slowly

sails, end over end, the length
of a block and arrives at last
upon the head of a sleeping

white Labrador, gold upon white
framed in deep purple light;

a lad bends over the dog;
with youthful reverence, he
whispers an awe-filled, "Cool."

MEDITATION OF AN OLD MAN STANDING ON A BRIDGE

Leaves fall in a slow spiraling drift, years pass almost
unnoticed until suddenly decades have vanished, life's pages

turn with an inevitable rhythm; even the wildest moments
of joy and passion are now infused with grief; we silently
lament beauty's loss, the rending of intelligence, the dimming

of wit, the harshness seeping into laughter, disappearance
of hope and faith, turning of eyes to stare towards

the dark maw yawning before us, creeping steadily
in our direction; when younger we imagined futures filled
with butterflies, blooming flowers, bouquets of love,

and a promise life had no limitations save those we chose to accept;
now joy is too often found in moments enshrined

in memory where light shines with an abundance
no longer found in the daily struggle to get from one task
to another, the effort to swim through grief to the other side

where acceptance allegedly awaits; too often the journey
merely deepens the pain of loss of parents, lovers, friends,

the smothering of the conviction that we are still capable,
still worthy of the time of others, still more than witness
to the epic that engulfs us all on our paths toward an end

none of us can fathom; night looms over the shoulder
of brightest day, and I turn to quiet moments

found in books, or music, or great works of art, or the still
beauty of forest, stream, garden, mountain soaring above,
or the discovery of an otter half-submerged in a creek

sending ripples in every direction, just as we send ripples
with every act we perform, good or bad, useful or valueless,

and every act of generosity (whether word, embrace,
smile, helping hand, or simple forgiveness) becomes a stay
against all that threatens the ability to survive the inevitable

fear, sense of loss, sinking into the pre-death of depression;
struggles to help others are therefore holy acts, acts by which

we help ourselves find moments that provide neither hope nor clarity,
nor surety that our lives have meaning, but are nonetheless
moments where we find beauty, find a kind of truth beyond

definition, a peace that eases (for a second or an hour) mind's clamor,
fills the darkness with light, eases our hearts for a brief time,

but then all we have is brief, all we know vanishes, and so
it seems good to quietly celebrate all that we can find which is worthy;
thus I can stare at streams of butterflies overhead and smile

at their journey, watch an egret fish and not mourn the fish caught,
but accept my part in life's cycle over which I have no control,

no understanding, no part to play beyond that of witness;
sanctus, sanctus, sanctus, holy is the ability to accept loss,
to face myself in the stream where the fish meets its fate and realize

(without anguish) I too will soon leave this world of sorrow and pain
and beauty and its moments of horror and joy inextricably intertwined.

A WET LATE AFTERNOON STROLL

my old eyes see a duck
in a swollen creek
no it's a log jutting up
and I am blind from age
and a driving rain
which blurs glasses

I stagger uphill
through wind and sleet
yet I am happier than I
have been in years
alone on darkening streets
wet from rain and sweat

and grateful that I can still
slog along whatever the conditions
amused by a bedraggled committee
of crows perched on power lines above
I shout don't you know enough
to get out of the rain

like most people they ignore me
a solitary truck passes
splashes me with a wave of street water
normally I would roar with curses
today it is simply another obstacle
triumphantly overcome

a heron is poised on a tree stump
an otter swims on his back
beneath water's surface
creates ripples which chart his path
in the distance three deer graze
in a backyard garden

and I drift through approaching
evening which drapes me
with a dark wet suit
which fits perfectly in the gloaming
and I disappear slowly through a shadowy door
which has been waiting for years

A SOMBER BEAUTY

Rain softly falls through bare branches;
wind whispers an accompaniment; thunder
unleashes distant rolls of tympani;

the evening sun's molten
oars of light
ignite your hair and set cheeks aflame

while falling water streams down your face
and your hair wild, dangerous, and replete
with promise flows toward deepest night.

I barely breathe...

...AND THERE'S AN END TO IT

You think the years will crest
and you'll surf down the other side
to thunderous applause
then step off into the backwash
and with quiet dignity
topple slowly backwards into waves,
an elegant withdrawal
complete with nod and serene smile
before disappearance into undertow;

but no, there is no
crest, no high drama,
no moment of recognition
validating all the petty struggle,
endless self-justification, crippling routine;
there is only this moment and the next
and the next and so forth
until there is no next

and all around the place
you had been treading water
no one notices there is one less
until a long time has passed and
someone asks, "Wasn't he (or she) here
just a moment ago? Where did he vanish to? Wasn't she just here?"
And certain people agree and others don't
and so the matter is settled
until someone looks around and another
is no longer there and so forth and so on and ...

I AM STILL LISTENING

an old saxophonist who could no longer play

sat through a concert of young musical studs
who blew the roof off the building

they musically inhabited they were bound
by no rules no limitations of form instruments
or imagination all was possible and they did not

care who could follow what they did

the old man who could no longer play loved
their chaotic joy their merger of anger exultation

wild exploration and whispered possibilities
when the group finished and stormed offstage
there was wild applause then everyone left

to find a bar somewhere save the ancient

who sat there nodding his head with a half-smile
on his face an acquaintance asked him to join

his group for a drink the old chap gently waved
him away and said just leave me for a while
I am still listening to that last sax solo it won't

stop talking to me don't worry I am feeling fine

WATERBOUND

I am a lover of rivers, their fierce
and gentle currents, broken branches
drifting downstream, their vessels
(canoes, rowboats, steamers, freighters,
passenger boats, tugboats, all

that use the river to enrich men's lives);
I sing songs and tell tales (true, invented,
borrowed from others), and have spent hours
sitting on riverbanks wondering what it is like
to live in the water, to move like a fish,

seabird, otter, have wondered what it is like
to wander free from rules of mankind,
to experience rain as simply part of a river;
even in sleep, I remember rivers, and dream
I am simply another denizen of the world of water.

LIFE AS A FOLK SONG

ho daddy ho
can't jump start the words
locked up tight
garaged in my smoky throat

jenny dang the weaver
who wove my feelings
into this labyrinth
where no light goes

no lark in the morning ever flew
higher than my dreams no wounded bird
dropped into deeper grass than my mind
when hope vanished along a winding road

no orphan train pulled a heavier load
than my feet shuffling through a mountain pass
toward the ocean where waves
would rock me in the cradle of life

just another wayfaring stranger
docking in your harbor loan me
a compass and I'll be on my way
the river be wide and I have days to cross

just a drifting log rolling and bobbing
one day picking some old dance tune
on your banjo you'll look around a corner to see
me knocking splinters loose from your rickety door

we'll find a shady grove and forget these
prodigal years a long time traveling a long time gone
give us a drink of water and let's stretch out
to watch the wind that shakes the barley

WHERE IS DISCOVERY FOUND
(listening to Miles near a stand of trees)

how many he seems to ask
how many
notes do you need
to make your horn sing
to lure listeners' feet into fleet
discoveries of joy and pain
the player knows a sparsity of sound
can turn one's soul round and round
in celebration of beauty found deep within
ah, too often my life fills with chagrin
but when horn or bird sings
my mind and heart take wild wing
and I whisper to all I love let us praise praise
praise all there is as life blazes

BIOGRAPHY

Michael L. Newell was born in Florida in 1945. In addition to living in thirteen states, he has lived in Japan, The Philippine Islands, Thailand, The United Arab Emirates, Jordan, Kuwait, Uzbekistan, Mexico, Egypt, Estonia, Saudi Arabia, Bolivia, and Rwanda. He currently lives in a small town on the Florida coast.

Newell studied writing with Benjamin Saltman and Ann Stanford. His poems have appeared in a number of periodicals including *Aethlon: The Journal of Sport Literature*; *Bellowing Ark*; *College English*; *Current*; *English Journal*; *First Class*; *The Iconoclast*; *Issa's Untidy Hut*; *Jerry Jazz Musician*; *Lilliput Review*; *Poetry Depth Quarterly*; *Rattle*; *Shemom*; *Ship of Fools*; *Tulane Review*; and *Verse-Virtual.*

Some of his previous books include *A Stranger to the Land*; *Seeking Shelter*; *A Long Time Traveling*; *Collision Course*; *Traveling without Compass or Map*; *Meditation of an Old Man Standing on a Bridge*; *Wandering*; *Each Step a Discovery*; *Making My Peace*; *The Harry Poems*; *Don't Fret (Jazz Poems)*, and *Still the World Beckons*.

www.ingramcontent.com/pod-product-compliance
Lightning Source LLC
Chambersburg PA
CBHW031522180726
48282CB00056B/225